REFLECTIONS
OF
A
MIND

PERSPECTIVE POETRY OF OUR BEING

GURMEET SINGH

PREFACE

Think These Things

Sail this with an open mind and a closer heart.
Keep it as a crosshair.
Keep your guns in the holster and your bullets aside.
As I take you to revisit by-lanes of memory
and thought.

Think this like the propellers of a barge.
Keep it as a smooth glide in the sea.
As new navigation of the thinker.

Think this to become the thinker.
To be the process of it all.
Keep it like an onward journey of the rough seas.
Take me as a rookie sailor.

Contents

IV

INTRODUCTION

Reflections of a mind is an observation of the mind and heart.

An idea that plays around our pre-beliefs of society and our mind-made systems. It's a concoction of poetry and perspective thinking. You'll experience a modest journey of my thoughts like a ship or a barge, as you may feel. It's about roughness and the beauty of life. A large part of this attempt is merely to show you the power of the mind and its thought.

I started compiling my work in 2019 and it's been an insightful journey. It's purely based on transparent thinking; a small celebration of my brain. A little of its own house party. I sometimes call it meditation.

This is for everyone who believes in mind matters and its command on the wellness of our existence. It's about seeing powers and the misbehaviours of our thoughts. Pain, Pleasure, Conflict, and Love.

All of this has one origin, The Mind.

Poetry is not about power,
but dispossession of it.
It needs a contemplation of your unruly spirit.
When you unbutton your mind,
and undress its precious pennies.
To perforate itself, to strip it to the skin.
When you stop hearing,
You feel calmness from the chaos.

When you retry and fail to recite your story.
When you struggle to scout your speech.
When you're startled to face the crowds.
You begin a search for your voice.
You will start making your own poetry.

TO EVERYONE AT
THE COAST

Wandered like a painter's piece,
Like an untouched canvas.
I din't belong there, nor in the mind of his.
I gazed until the stars went strong.
I lusted for desires and wrath for peace.
The greed of the greens, none were mine.

Don't take me as my colour.
I don't belong to any.
The strokes of hopes, games, and thrones;
nor the dynasties were mine.

Don't take me as an answer.
I don't believe in any.
Not in the questions from the captain.
I'm not robust, nor do I fear the wind.
I'm only navigating my barge.
So, I could tell everyone at the coast.
Not all those who wander are lost.

23-04-2020

WE STARTED DREAMING

Today is a matter of breath and its hold.
An idea we built in our minds.
An alliance of today and tomorrow.
We named it hope.
An unseen journey of the mind.
A voyage from our bearings to our desired harbours.
We called it ambition.
In reality, we're at war with future,
Making it grand and glorious.
We dream like Kings.
Behave like misers.
There isn't a throne.
Isn't a kingdom to amass.

Only a force within.
A wave of endless thoughts and illusions.
A creed of power and passion to build inside.
For you to break it as many times.
And call it Dreams.

RISE AND FALL

We come with surprises.
Fighting to take place, we celebrate.
Rising to crawl, stumbled to fall.
Growing up to hold these walls.
We trust in the corners of a home.
We rise again, to fall again, to hold again.
Every time to different walls.

We face fears we never had.
We think things that don't exist.
Lost in this world to find love, that one soul.
We forget to give, take what's given, accept what's chosen.
Yet we rise and fall.

We doodle every day.
Laugh at pranks and brawls.
Pushing our despairs up the walls.
Yet we rise and fall.

We give birth again with memories and joy.
We find a face to the fetus; we call it life again.
To hold the same walls, to fall and crawl again.
Yet we rise and fall.

04-08-2019

THE BOHEMIAN HEART

This is my bohemian house.
There are art and culture.
Coupled with my duties and upright posture.
My old-wood mom-made rusted table.
Turquoise beads in corridors.
A quaint smell of plants and weed.

Stuffed with local literature and woody coffees.
Threads falling in between the doors.
Cushions on the floor had tiny mirrors, said tiny tales.
Some had visitors, some stayed.
The music was faint, almost none for the pets.
There kept a dairy open with love – it said.
Covered in leather and feathers or so.

Most of it was empty not one.
The last one had finished ink-like marks.
Anxious words by the end of a drag.
A dry mouth and a stronger heart.
Halfway through the crease, a small paper hanging – said,
This is my bohemian heart.

BELONGINGS

Forget that we belong anywhere.
What's mine can never be yours and likewise.
I can't claim love until the truth is true.
True in all sense, honest as one.

To be all in.
To trust in the plays and lose all the roulettes.
To grow a great source within.
Be slow and candid, that's when it'll mean a lot.

Forever doesn't prevail, nor for you or me or this planet.
The stars too break.
What's going to last forever.
A belonging to you and all of me.

02-09-2019

ATTACHED STRINGS

Hear the violin and its strings.
Feel the tremors of its chords.
Trying to show something.
An admission, a synergy.
Telling us a story of the soul.

This wooden beast shows us how to love.
Love like it, for it needs a placid balance.
Staring at the eyes of its neck—
Just like a dangerous kiss.

Improvising in consent and accord.
Where no strings are attached.
Yet they strike a chord.

DENIALS

Denials today can root conflicts of tomorrow.
Hidden treasures are dusted after time.
To accept will ensure us to battle and bout.
To let go of disuse and its residues.

We'll face pain as a part of dismissal,
With the power of acceptance.
Denial and its demons won't exist.

It's as simple as water flowing in the seas.
As sharp as a sailor's eye.
Showing us what's within and the tough storms
that made us.

12-09-2019

WHERE IS THE LOVE

Love is hidden, beneath everything.
It's withering off like leather and skin.
It's something roses cannot give.

It's in the lines of unspoken poetries.
And a lot more than words cannot say.

It's all that we live to smile and giggle.
To howl and roar, to moan and show, to tie or to fold.
Its everything we consume to damage and kill.
Love is still,everything you cannot see.

WHAT LIES BENEATH

What lies under
Is a cave of control.
A wave of confessions.
A block of emotions.
Paradoxes and possessions.
A story of conflicts.
Solace and solutions.

What lies above
Is the glory of the lords.
Ballads and beauties.
Esteem and confidence.
Display and demeanour.
Smokes of the fire within.
Heart and expression.

CHARIOTS OF THE SPIRIT

Spirit's like a carriage.
A vehicle that drives our actuality in full.
We do it all in the guidance.
It's our conscience and gratitude.
Our psyche and its enemies.
The feed to the spirit is an eventual result of us.

The skills of our morale lie in,
Staring at the sun, wondering at constellations.
Closing our eyes to hear the silence.
And when the fears arrive.
That's our spirit.

THOUGHT KNEW IT ALL

Even if I was a pirate and knew all my stars
I'd be still finding gold in the sea.
I still wouldn't be on land,
Till I waited for the brightest stars, in the darkest nights.
And they could guide me home.

Even if I was a monster and knew all my powers.
I'd still be weak in my knees when I saw my mother.
I wouldn't feel her soreness and love.
Until I sat her down again.
She was the strongest of them all,
The only one to make me fragile again.

Even if I was a saint and knew all my prayers.
I'd still be asking God for rosaries and favours.
I wonder if I can find him at all.
He told me to look around.
Only till I gathered; he's at home.
And I din't know it at all.

26-04-2020

LOVE AT ITS BEST

Love is best bewitched and insane.
How does it remain like that?
How can we love in grandeur?
Like royals and the majesties.
How can we untie the knots from it?
How does it remain like that?

Wild, silly, and wacky.
Just like the first arouse.
Trust and honor, the christened pillars of it
Are too anaemic.
We stand too tall with our egos on it.
Ripping them from the bedrock of it.

Breaking them all, one by one.
Just like an old building collapses.
Searching memories from the rumbles.
And only when it's ground zero again
Love is at it's best again.

SECRET PASSAGE

I have a secret passage.
Sometimes I lose the keys.
I often find them with a secret message.
I remember it on most days.
Sometimes I blank out.
I remind myself, till I don't realize.
Sometimes people remind me of my path.

I find closures with no meanings.
Sometimes I find meanings with no closures.
I found tools in my treasure box.
Bliss, charm, and contentment.
There was also sadness and defeats, over nothing
but simple truths.
Sometimes I smile over silly things.
Silly things, which are simple truths.

I found a path to my treasure box,
It was my own forgotten message.
Which had people and their simple truths.

24-04-2020

BROKEN LADDERS

Came here alone.
Climbed a million stairs.
Slipped so many times.
Fell to ground zero.
Fought many battles.
Lost so many of them.
Came back up for a better flight.
They asked me to rebuild again.
Failed so many times.
Reached up here to feel the altitude.
They tried to break my ladder.
Wishing a great fall.
With every step I took, I found a broken piece.
So, I decided to fly.

COMING HOME

Coming home has stronger arrival.
It's got an underlying warmth.
An unsaid responsibility.
Satisfaction of an awkward power.
A resistance of your own chair.
It's a madness of your jungle.
It's the inner realm of quiescing and peace.

Knowing your anarchies and demons.
Home is accepting your wars and awards.

When you're arriving close to the bindings.
Mastering your defaults and smiles.
That's when you're coming home.

10-09-2019

THE VOICE

I believed in a germ.
A process of a voyage.
In the storms that took me down.
The waves that lifted me up.

I trusted; there is an army inside.
I regarded my crashes and the arrears.
I confided in the stars when they showed up.
I looked at the sun when it all went down.
And the moon when it got all dirty and divided.

I believed in the fireworks when life exploded.
Even in those who disbelieved.
Some who showed up.
I was kept alive in their memory.
Some who gifted a brick to my stature.
I stood alone in my fights and fractures.
And all the signs I couldn't speak.
So, I just believed a voice in me.

INDEPENDENCE DAY

Freedom isn't designed for hoists and flags.
As to what freedom really is.
A Blunt satisfaction.
A stillness of vengeance.
A fight to see our caged fears.

Freedom is not in desire or substances.
Nor in memoir or triumphs.
It's not in parades or bows.
Nor in anthems or stiff toes.

It's not an event for the scuffled pastors.
It's an end to our riffs within.
For it's to strike our fears with powers.

It's a re-fill to the craters we created.
To believe, there isn't a finale to all this blood and glory.

Freedom is to see refinements.
To destroy internal paradoxes.
It's to be aware.
Freedom is to live clear and close to all you cannot see.

                    14-08-2019

FUTURE, A ROTTEN STAR

Clutch so much for later.
For the best is yet to come—they said.

Don't like the fragments of today.
Love the granules of tomorrow.

Future is hollow in its essence. Has no demeanor.
He's an assassin of an era's soul.

He makes you breathe in half.
His very own stench decomposes your hold.

Today has a deeper scent.
She has a stronger aroma.
She is intimate.
Unlike, the far future you cannot even touch.

Living for the current trends.
Seeking destiny and its jeopardies.

We can't keep the angels of hope,
Alongside the demons of future.

Besides, Future is a rotten star.
His brightness is a command of her,
For future he's is only a slave, by order of today.

JUNGLE RULES

Only jungles have decrees.
Cities have charts to trace.
Loins roar with no fright.
Man fears society and other men.

The jungle is an intimate setting,
An unguarded scene.
While no one watches over,
They stick to tribes and prides.
Waiting for the sunset.
And the game begins.

We haven't learnt from the jungle,
To stop defending our façade-pride.
To heed unity and its valence.
Displace when needed.
Watch the sun rise.
As in the cities, we grow older.
And game ends.

05-09-2019

LET IT BE

Leave it as is to outgrow you,
Allow it to make it home.
Cease itself, contained and captured.
Handcuffed and motionless.
Stand upright with stillness.

A struggle to push will drag it further.
An act to get over will destroy your anchor.
Breathe in with a full hoard of faith.
Seek with power to recover.

You'll need pain as a process of it.
You'll need an oracle – as is.
Won't heal if it's covered,
Even wounds heal quicker, uncovered as is.

THE MUSIC ROOM

This is my musical room.
I visualize music; it looks great.
That's a magical repair, a fix for the flux.
To unthink the box, to tie a full thought.
To amend and break down your virtues.
To reconcile and smile in your blues.

The chords of a jazz song, the notes of a guitar.
The voice, trying to announce its avatar.
Feel the thrills and the quiets.
Giving rights to your reservoirs.

Creates a poise for a confession you never gave.
Bracing you to like life and its notes.
Healing you to like you and not your hopes.

06-08-2019

BETTER MINDS

To a better mind.
There would be layers.
Just like an onion.
You'll need a peel.
To know the centre of you.
Underlying statements.
For which you never read because you never saw.

An eye of depth.
A seabed of erosions.
Like a true passing hurricane.
Like a new genre of eruptions.

A fresh phenomenon.
To open the mind with static.
To get beneath the layers of you.
To evacuate what's decoyed,
To bear off the lowest of you.

OWN ROADS

It was never an option.
Din't even mean to be.
An uneven road that wasn't potential.
To creep till here in a colossal way.
A puny nudge from a prior place.
Brings me the heroism to leap.
To stride to a road, that wasn't sealed for me.

The only power I asked—was the power to think.
Never wished a priceless painting.
Never was easy to catch a rising sun.
Never had those bellyful nights to dream the day.

It was that ounce of courage, to think.
I could make my own road one day.

21-09-2019

MADNESS

I proudly looked in the mirror.
A screaming stare in her eyes.
A mediation like a clear film.
A madness to the countdown.

I could see the fluorescent.
I could talk her down —I was the only one.
I was the one with control.
Only I could catch her craze.

Where no one could,
I could see the world.
It only was her, who carried me there.

PROMISE NOT TO FALL

Promise not to fall,
Promise to stand tall.
Allow the sandstorms.
Burn up the fires with fury.
Keep up to the promises and glory.
Commit to the sun and its shine.
Be soft like the moonlight.
Allow the autumn.

Touch the sky with grace.
Be a pioneer at your turn.
Be a star of your time.
Allow to break and burn.

Try to fly if wings were tapered.
Take a higher flight.
Come down if you have to.
Break down if you need to.

Stay still but,
Promise not to fall.

29-08-2020

SIMPLE LOVE

I look at simple love.
I don't understand the pillars of faith.
The Pressures of bonding.
Chores of trust.
Promises of loyalty.

I look for clear eyes, like crystals.
So, I can see through everything I can.
For all the answers I need.

I'm only staring at you, so close to me.
To let you be.
So, test everything I can.
For you to be you and for me to be me.

DESTINATION

It matters the most when you think.
When you stay involved in thought,
As a whole and not a moment.
When you adapt and accept your nuisance,
Therapy begins then.

When you see darkness as night and not as noir.
It matters the most.
When you see the mind as power and not its choir.

Its atrocious monkeys and a qualified monk.
It matters the most when u think.
When you see thought as a source,
and not as a destination.

09-08-2019

POWER OF SILENCE

I achieved silence.
With no foot stomps or armies.
An opera in my ears.
And no circles of dreams.

I achieved stillness.
With a static on the ropes and a rainbow in my eyes.
I saw rays of hope.
Pushing me to find pace, I wasn't willing.
I loved the slow and I wasn't planning.

I achieved resilience.
A cover to self, to get beneath my source.
To find the universe I came for.
To see the nature, I live for.

I achieved freedom.
Freedom of them all.
I believed in the riots of liberty and its moralities.
I created a warfare within — with no artilleries.
The strongest army always remained silent – they said.

This battle was over, long ago.
With the misleads of freedom.
And the power of silence.

SHOOTING STAR

I can't see the lights go off.
Don't want the sun to go down.
Don't like the stars to drip.
Although I love the moonlight.

I know, I have to face the dusk.
I know, I want the endless love.
I know, I can find my way to the celestials.
Although I'll need blackness of the burns.

I know, I shouldn't be scared of evil.
Nor be worried about the dark knight.
I know, I'll be with the skies soon.

I know, I'll break into a million pieces.
Although I love a shooting star.

05-09-2019

WHY I DREAM

Connected to an outer space.
Kept me away from the muddle.
Said hello to my beasts and baits.
Got closer to my demons and saints.

Saw a lake full of petals, mountains full of snow.
A barren land cracked open my ground below.
Showed me my nasty beneath and perfections above.

Touched a pair of polar lights.
I stitched a planet of T-Rexes too.
Bought the damn stars.
I saw an aphrodisiac too.

I painted mirrors of my desires.
I saw my own colour. It was black and grey.
Red and white with pink all over.
Smudged in blues of my greed all over.

Fired my intensities.
Warned and escorted—also re-frightened.
Click by click, I broke and reformed.
I opened my eyes,
And I saw a dream happen.

FOREVER'S FREEDOM

At first,
We don't understand freedom.
It comes at our worst times.
When we're at the lowest and bare-chested.

It comes,
When we're bruised and busted.
When there's nothing to lose.

Free of fear.
Bullet-proofed within.

Not held captive from a mind.
That's when we're free from within.
Forever.

22-09-2019

IGNORANCE IS NO BLISS!

Ignorance is not bliss.
Roses too possess unfelt barbs.
Apathy, a weapon to mankind.
Unawareness, like explosive undermines.

Ignorance, a medal to hide a voice.
A poor inward expertise— to address, to caress.
To talk to a nation.
A tomb, or to save a creature.

Severing to believe a perceived story.
A well-rehearsed self-banter, a monologue with glory.
Frequently used as shields with no holes.
Counting no damages to the heart and souls.

OBSESSIONS

What makes us obsess?
On Humans, Love and Wealth?
Cleanliness and thoughts?
The mind goes a bit nutty-curious.
Curious to find its pleasures.
Pleasures of pain and proprietary.

Leaves a mark on-self—It claims.
Creates problems and its places.
Finds a believed motive and its traces.
Thrives on conclusions and its unfinished races.

Obsessions are of pursuits.
Pursuits of happiness and possessions.
Forging a crazy state of undeath.

A blessing from the greed of all.
During Obsessions and its WWIIIs,
We missed our presence and
The mind didn't know it at all.

JEALOUSY

Jealousy has no substance.
It can't hold itself. It's powerless.
A concept of inward imbalance.
A misconception of the other.

It feasts on fleshes of attention and care.
A feeding system to our central side.
It talks to our alert mind.
Hints, Grass is gold on the other side.

Jealousy and anger, both are friends of another—
Their friendship is at the mercy of imagery.
The best-looking angle we created.
A perfect inner misery.
None of the upper crusts and royals,
Get the last rights of one's reality.

WATER

Get inspired by water.
An ocean isn't powerful in itself.
A river doesn't flow by itself.
There isn't a lake or reservoir without water.

Water's like a thought.
A thought that could create.
Create your spirit or sound.
An emotion or euphoria –
Just like meditation.

Watch this liquid inside of you.
Let it stir, the soul of you.

STAR WARS

We only appear in the dark when it's cordial and quiet.
We never left.
Only covered by a Sun.

We mean a lot.
We give direction.
We invented planets.

We got you home from the lost lands.
We burst and dropped from higher heights.

We got hit by stranger things.
We faced the storms in space.

Yet we showed up every night,
Yet we twinkled, every day.

We also broke and fell.
We also rose and shined.

WALKING ON WATER

An intimate window, a weird kind of smell.
No friction in the woods.
Made a strange kind of noise.
An unruly voice within.
Touched a centre chest weird place.
Beneath my tongue— was a small gulp in.
A gulp of insecurity.
A door that small, could I get in?
Wasn't so clear a thought, wasn't so bold of a move.
The stakes were clear, I had to take a leap.
A leap of torn faith and memoir.
I wasn't wrong, there was a story— behind that door.

A story of a young boy dreaming— like he always did.
A crazy place, full of chaos.

He dreamed of the universe and its artistry.
Places of water, fire,and ice.
A sight he saw never before.
Wasn't strong to climb a tree.

Went to the waters alone, like always before.
Dreamed, like he always wanted to,
Walked on water, like he always wanted to.

02-05-2020

FIRST TIME

I thought we were spelled to be.
Enough to last a lifetime.
An era of you and me.
The first time I saw a dissection.
Rattling reflections of tries,
Ease of cries.

Blamed myself, not you.
To sting myself, not you.
I lost desire.
Desire in you, not me.
First, I learned to release.
Release thoughts and not you.

This time I reposed.
Early practiced to forget.
It was the first time I learnt,
How you looked the first time, I saw you.

PURPOSES

Purpose, like an agenda?
An idea of completion or plans?

A purpose can't be defined,
Nor be undertaken or refined.

I relate purpose to light.
Something you don't plot or routinise.

A voice from within; a song from the past.
Has no thought to criticise.

It's a numbness for madness.
A selfless activity you do it for the light,
Only you can see.

Something you believe because they will.
So, you're the source; thereby you're the purpose.

SEPARATED ILLUSIONS

Separation comes with illusions.
A completion of a lifecycle or tenure.

It's the breaking that hurts.
The feeling of losing a heart.
A perception of being mortal.

Separation is our progress.
An evolution of us.
A new chapter in our nodes.
Like a snake deskins the scales and holes.
Like wildebeest in African fields.
Just like the northern lights disappear.
Just like parted souls don't reappear.

Until you part ways for a better you.
Until you rejoin with a new self to shed again.
To become you again.

FEAR EYES

Feared eyes.
Scared to fall in.
Terrified of heights and falls.
Tightly netted with the sharks.

Couldn't bury this timidity?
Or make it a valence.
Couldn't dab onto these dreads?
Or infatuate stronger heads?

Dreams too ferocious to be scared of.
Faced shrapnel and the spikes of rust.
What's going on with Hope?
A raw trust.

A pair of fearful eyes, like the Jaguar.
Promises made, like a Cheetah's claw.

Like the heat of his body.
Aware of his patterns.
I could convert my fears
Into fearless battles.

24-07-2019

WATCH THE MIND

Watch the mind perform for you.
In a grand concert.
Like Beethoven's symphony of 100 musicians.
All playing various instruments.
All in time and sync.
Watched by the conductor himself.

BLAME GAME

Blame isn't a game.
But a hallucination of choices.

A fetish play of defeats and vices.
Domination of positions.
A delusion of reality and its pieces.

What's meant to be will always be.
You could blame it on the time or its sequences.

BEAUTIES OF BEING LOST

Being lost has beauty.
A sharp shame of clarity.
The purity of darkness, it's black, so it's clear.
At full to seek out, you'll find a personality.

Being confused is intense.
Hopes to decide and choose.
It's the grey matter.
Chances are you'll lose a character.

Being lost is a powerful homecoming.
To move a barge in the rough tides.
To find shores in the wild seas.
Till you face your failing trumpets.
Till you conclude your pursuits of happiness.

REFORM

There's a gorgeous beauty in reform.
It's life telling you to turn off the heat,
Before it burns.

An uncertain scare.
Dangling decisions, Questioning actions.
Come together in reformed perfections.

When you're breaking—almost born.
Shattering—almost gone
That's when you'll be reformed.

29-02-2020

FAITH PHENOMENA

Faith is a phenomenon.
Like a blind man to his darkness.
You can have faith in mineral and mountain,
call them your God.
Create a cult to believe, you are the God.

Faith is easy, like an idea.
Gets going with a thought.
Turns into belief and blocks.
You could have faith in many ways.
Believe in Buddhism or be carried away.
Washed by Terrorism or its brutal ways.

It's a silver lining of the mind,
Of things you can't envision.
A passion for endless trajectories,
Guiding your gut and vision.

As Power cannot be built without faith,
Faith can't be built without power.

SECURE SURENESS

We seek sureness.
Sureness with flair.
Hardly slept in faith and colour.
Made a note of everything great and rare.

Perfections altered.
Stitching fitter versions, to suit us, in our way.
Doubled attempts to be measured again.
Just to be sure,
To be bloodedly loved and not hung again.

Loving with mannequins and avatars—we made them best
in grades.
At last,
A dye of their faces in the shades of us.
Just to be secure of their sureness in us.

02-09-2019

RECIPES OF THE SUN

Make your own sun and stare at it.
Think about your stars.
Be your moon and the craters of it.

Can't fail your power to blaze.
Can't doubt your force to fire.
Don't trust makers of the rules.

Break them to recreate.
Be nuclear.
Be the radical power of it.

Let us recreate our galaxies.
And all the routes of it.

Let us stare at the stars every day.
Let us bring them down every day.

BECOMING WARRIOR

To believe in yourself.
To trust and not doubt an ounce.
To be weak, to be strong.
To cry, to be emotional.
To express, to be grateful.
To fight against the wrong.
To mediate for the calmness of the mind.
To battle with stillness.
To create a still moment, to overcome the evil voice.
To reign the mind, to let it loose.
To surrender to sadness.
To rejoice to happiness, to celebrate life.
To believe sadness is a part.
To love endlessly, to not hide, but to show.
To be hurt to be complete.

29-09-2019

WHAT IS TO LOVE

We yearn to be loved like a boomerang, not a bullet.
Coming back in more vengeance.
Deeper depths and higher isolations.

We love in levels.
Love shouldn't need high rises.
No fancy facades.
Only a stairway with no exits.

It's better to be a frontline soldier.
Not afraid by a bullet, only to aim and fire.
With more power and fewer protections.

CHASING TIME

Chasing Time—The biggest champion.
Might miss or pass out an age.
Chasing people and dominions.
Emplacements and Oracles of rage.

Destroys an origin or a core.
It's the same for the rich or poor.
We remained kings of our domains.
Built castles for our queens.

In the end.
A battlefield of deceased.
Flags and territories—there were regions and treaties.
Time's the biggest champion.
Stayed still with newer fantasies and dreams.

CLOUDS & DOUBTS

Dark clouds do prevail.
For they carry a strong message.
They signal us hailstorms and rains.
Unlike doubts carry agony and aches.

Skies clear as the sun is up.
You can rise with intuitions.
With arms wide open and
Great knowledge of aches.

FOLICIES OF UNDOING

We spent time.
Trying to undo our priors of society and so on.
Our truth was limited from the eons.

A mere attempt of,
Fixing our past with the present.
We blocked fresh air.
Breathed short to memorize wrong shots.
Called it new to avoid hopes.

With every breath.
A brand-new script.
Like every tide has its own time.
I had to choose my depths and dangers.
So, I counted every second as new time.

25-08-2019

TACTICS OF HOPE

Another day passed in agony.
Many afternoons spent being distant.
In insight and amid, I wondered.

Another big night-in, bantering the regulars.
Blaming the rulers.
Being hostage to stay put. It was captive.

Closing my eyes to waking up.
To what I needed the most — It was Hope.

(Written during Covid-19 Lockdown. Mumbai. India)

MALFUNCTIONS

Audacities driving malfunctions.
Over-conscious of what others reckon.
Don't like to be old and raunchy.
Don't like the skin giving up on me.
Also, the greys aren't that fancy.

Constantly high on staying fresh and young.
With all unique prepositions.
Not agreeing with my faults and functions.

Only to smother our divinity.
We made these predictions.
To forget a prior, we gathered in order.
Mastered the act of humanity.

Never focused on our malfunctions.
Always dumbfound at game point.
Never could serve any aces - unlike Federer.
No cups, no gold, no podiums.
Stood there with no practice.
Never fixed our malfunctions.

09-09-2019

VICTORY NEVER WON

Winning is not about victory.
It's strife within.
Nor the defeats are glorious.

Ending wars in remains were never victorious.
Victory is just a name.
A hand to hand combat.
Winning is a judgment of the game.

When you hear the silence of the mind.
Super-powers, Gurus,and God-men—and all that we
follow,
Are the generals of our own hollows.
While a victory is a throne of stillness within.

MY FRIENDS

My friends are here.
Not all of them.
Some could make it, some could not.
Some have deeper pockets than I could ever have.
Some have bigger hearts than I could ever give.

Some do a lot for me, more than I can for them.
Some drive me crazy, most of them.
They think of me as theirs.
They stood by me as they were mine.

Some met me halfway but stayed longer.
Some left midway and came back here.

Here they are to accept me, how I am.
I had many choices to betray them.
I had to choose a few old to hold with.
And a few new to part with.

29-08-2019

IT'LL BE DUST

It'll all be dust, very soon.
The dusk of dawn.
The starry nights.
It'll disappear in a tomb.

The shores will be washed away.
Sandcastles will dissolve in a moment.
We could be in ashes and grey.

From stones to pebbles, it'll all decay.
The mountains will come down at last.
Cold airs in the forests will burn like grenades.
We'll be dust of the past, very soon.

For the feelings, they will always be.
The emotions will always remain.
For everything that is gone.
The heart will still take its chance.
To beat again, very soon.

LESSER DREAMS

On no account, dream less.
You can soar a flight.
Don't think less.
You can fight the hounds.
Keep your dreams around.

Give it your highest altitude.
Every trickle of your thought.
Every strike of your heart.

You can want more, till you end.
Never fly low.
You can extend your wings afar.
Don't be scared of the last wing, even if it's broken.

You can rebuild more.
You can cry or break more.
You can succumb to the ground if you have to.
You'll be crystallized for all you know.

Let the fears, fire your wings.
Be voluptuous if you have to.
Don't be small in things.
Don't accept a lesser dream.
A dream cannot have a size,
Only if you don't measure its wings.

                                        23-04-2020

THERE IS NO EPILOGUE

There is no ending.
We never started to end; we want to last forever.
Maybe this is our plan.
Newer things that we dream of, excite us.

Now, if a dream gave us an infinite source of possibilities.
A galaxy of endless thoughts.
Newer versions of ourselves.
How can that ever end?

We wake up to a new thought every day.
We rethink new ideas every day.
There's only a start.
A new push to reach the finish line.
A dream can never have a photo finish.
How can it ever die?

This is our epilogue of the beginning.
A grand curtain raiser of our show.
To all the small things in our boat.
We start here because you reached here,
With the reflections of a mind.

23-04-2020

THANK YOU

www.ingramcontent.com/pod-product-compliance
Lightning Source LLC
Chambersburg PA
CBHW031333130726
47988CB00007B/3102